CALIFORNIA PALMS

A Collection of Short Stories

CALIFORNIA PALMS

A Collection of Short Stories

Marnell Jameson

Sunstone Press
Santa Fe, New Mexico

First Edition

Printed in the United States of America

Library of Congress Cataloging in Publication Data:

Jameson, Marnell, 1960-
    California palms, a collection of short stories / by Marnell Jameson. —
1st ed.
        p.   cm.
    Contents: The art of being neighborly — Shadows -- The legacy — Peace
time — Facade — Summer school — The gas station.
ISBN: 0-86534-140-0 : $8.95
    I. Title.
PS3560.A398C3   1990
813'.54--dc20   89-49518
                                                                    CIP

Published in 1990 by SUNSTONE PRESS
                    Post Office Box 2321
                    Santa Fe, NM 87504-2321 / USA

To my parents

CONTENTS

The Art of Being Neighborly / 9

Shadows / 19

The Legacy / 33

Peace Time / 47

Facade / 51

Summer School / 65

The Gas Station / 79

THE ART OF BEING NEIGHBORLY

Lucerne Lane is a quiet street, a California cul-de-sac, where people raise families, settle, retire. Dichondra lawns grow purely, without effort, unblemished by rye and dandelions, and yards look as if they're manicured with tweezers. After the garbage men come, retired men sweep the gutters to keep themselves serviceable. And the neighbors clean up after their dogs. It is a street that lets nothing bad happen. Nothing ugly like drunken teenagers or burglars mars the surface of the serene landscape. And if it does, the offender is quietly chastised, the disruption ignored and buried so neatly as not to leave a trace.

My husband and I replaced a couple who had lived

in our house since it was built some 40 years back. We were new blood on the street, so we were watched suspiciously at first. But we learned quickly to keep our yard neat, our garage door closed, and our front door open. In order to assimilate, we practiced the art of being neighborly — graciously accepting homegrown lemons, avocados and zucchini; buying something, anything, at local garage sales, and making the requisite appearances at Tupperware gatherings and craft parties.

And we were especially careful to please our immediate neighbors Ted and Veneta (we privately called her Velveeta because she seemed so much like a product of process) because with them we shared a common wall and driveway. Velveeta was a predictable sort, always dressed as if she could leave for the country club, in her California-casual, usually designer sweats. Her two-year-old Seville bore a Marriage Encounter bumper sticker and had a hot-pink puff ball for a key chain. Every year before Christmas you could count on Velveeta to come collecting for the March of Dimes. She'd yell, "Yoo-Hoo," before ringing the bell, "Just any old change you've got in a sock."

She and Ted were old blood on Lucerne and old enough to be our grandparents. They adopted us and forgave us our youthful abruptness, because we were new and sparkling and clean.

I always sensed they wanted some of our life to spill over onto their property. I sometimes let it, but mostly I didn't. Mostly I tried to maintain that social balance between being outwardly interested and inwardly unattached, because I knew Ted and Velveeta, their type anyway. They were the kind who got involved, invested, with their long tap roots like the California palms that reach down to the center of the earth and grab hold. And who has time for that these days?

That was why when Ted invited us to a barbecue I made that excuse about my mother-in-law in the hospital. But we went anyway. We weren't that rude. And that mention about visiting hours and leaving early gave us an out. Nevertheless, it was awkward. There was this other "young couple," you see, and another "old couple." Balance, I guess. And the widow. The party was to make our acquaintance, a coming out for us, only we didn't want out. (And can those old folks drink.)

We didn't eat meat and were too polite to say anything before the dinner, so there was that uncomfortable moment when the hamburgers were served. Everyone just stared at our plates (filled with green salad, cream-cheese spread, beans and Ritz crackers) and felt the difference.

After dinner, we sat around the pool, where Velveeta had floated these funny plastic candle things.

The younger set listened to the elders talk old neighborhood stories. Like when June Juniper (that was really her name) had a psychic out to rid her house of ghosts, and when, at a white elephant party, some Hadley lady received as a gift the very Christmas ornament she'd made and given out the year before.

"Is that Frank Bradley's goat story you're telling?" Ted, who was fixing drinks at the bar, asked. He was a little hard of hearing.

"Oh, no. We're saving that one for you." The widow was always polite.

By the time we began our contrived exit, the older folks started this game of toasting to whatever notion rolled off their loosened tongues: "Here's to the family of plaster ducks on the lawn. May they have joy and prosper." Then they'd take a big swig, hoot with uproarious laughter and conjure another toast. The other young couple took slighter sips and were admirable in their feigned enjoyment.

As we said our good-byes, Ted put one fatherly hand around me, clutched a margarita glass the size of a fish bowl in the other and said: "My gawd, you're just a kid. Lift your glass, honey. Don't have one? Here." He handed me his. "Here's to all you have to drink to."

After that night, the pressure of being acquainted, of being more than neighbors rose, so that I felt guilty every time I had anyone over and not them. An embarrassing amount of time passed and I never returned their invitation, even though I meant to. But I did make a point to ask about their flowers when I met them out in front.

Usually this would happen when I was backing out of my driveway. I'd see Ted in his garden and he'd saunter over, so I had to stop, roll down my window and chat. I'd say something like how lovely the blossoms on his magnolia tree looked, and he'd say how busy I seemed always running in and out, and I'd latch on to the opportunity to say, as a matter of fact I'm late now for my ten o'clock appointment. And so, with a wave and a smile, I'd leave him standing in the driveway holding his gardening gloves thinking, probably, how he'd like to tell me about his youth.

In the mornings, out for my jog, I'd wave to the men out front collecting their newspapers. They wore full pajamas and knee-length plaid robes, which made me wonder about their sex lives, and whether they had twin beds like Jane Wyatt and Robert Young on "Father Knows Best."

And I'd often see the elderly widow walking her beagle. She carried a little shovel and a bag and had a bounce that made me feel like humming. I didn't remember her name, but she always said good morning as if she remembered mine. She was Ted's other

———

neighbor, and since her husband's death, Ted had taken out her trash each week, fixed her broken sprinkler heads, and taken over other heavy chores.

One day, as I was just heading out for my run, the widow asked me if she could take a cutting from the geraniums in my front yard. Of course, I said, as if she were a friend of my mother's from church. Sensing she wanted to chat, I hurried off. I was timing myself, you see, trying to do my five-point-five miles in less than forty-five minutes, and I wouldn't if I stood there talking, wasting time. I promised myself to ask her what she called her dog. But next time, not now.

It struck me, and I thought about it as I ran, that she still wore a gold wedding band on her bony, brown-freckled hand. Her skin didn't fit so well, and I wondered what it felt like being married to someone dead. Later, I was pleased to see the red geraniums blossom in that clay pot on her front porch. I knew they were well cared for.

We were having a dinner party the day Ted found her. I drove past the paramedic van parked in front of her house on my way to the grocery store. Pretending all was well, I nodded to the neighbors who stood in their front yards, at a socially correct distance, looking solemn. It was early, a Saturday, and many of them were still in their bath robes. I tried to forget the scene as I picked over fresh vegetables and read wine labels.

———

14

Everything had to be perfect at my little dinner party. We had invited my husband's business partner and his wife. They were both younger but not by much and had just that week moved into their first house less than a mile away.

Ted was out front when I got back. The other neighbors, not knowing what else to do, had gone inside. So he wouldn't keep me long, I carried two grocery bags as I went to ask what had happened. Maybe it was just a heart attack and the paramedics got there in time, I thought. Ted didn't even notice my arms were burdened, so I set my bags down on the curb grass, embarrassed by my petty scheme.

The July afternoon was smothering, a day most Californians spend running from air-conditioned house to air-conditioned car. The air stood still. Birds didn't move. Trees didn't breathe. Ted and I sat on the curb with our feet in the gutter as he told me how he found her.

"She was face down in a pool of blood," he said evenly in the monotone that comes in the aftermath of trauma. "She'd been there for three days, the coroner said. I'd noticed her mail and newspapers collecting and that's why I investigated. She was in the garage. And, you know," (I'll never forget his look, as if this were the most unjust part.) "still no one can tell whether she fell and died, or died and fell."

———

Her son would come in from Washington the next day, he went on. Her son. I never knew she had a son. Ted gave me details in no logical order. I asked no questions and I didn't know what to say, except I'm sorry. I had no right to grief. I deserved to feel nothing. I made myself forget about my groceries, my stupid dinner party, so for once I could let Ted talk.

And he did. He talked in a stream about the day she moved in more than thirty years ago. "Her son, little Mikey, ha! he's a big CPA now, carted boxes in on his wagon, and it was not too soon before he found the sprinklers. Boy, could she screech at him. You could hear her for miles, such a voice for a little lady. Always insisted on starting the songs at parties. We told her she was off-key, but that was no matter." Ted paused and rolled his bare head back till the hinge of his neck stopped it and he looked into the sky. "Darn you, Helen." The clouds seemed in no hurry as they drifted by in long streaks like tail feathers.

"Yeah, we had some wild times," he went on. "Some great parties, and she'd be telling jokes up to the end of the night, and she never complained the way the other women did when we threw her in the pool."

As he reminisced, his heart seemed to lift, and I saw him, through his coarse gray skin, as a younger man — his belly not quite so round — light and laughing, throwing women into pools, and elbowing

---

16

his pals in the ribs when he beat them at cards.

He stopped talking as they took the covered body out on a stretcher. He was rolling a piece of dichondra between his fingers, the crushed blade left his fingers moist and green. He put the stem in his mouth. Then the coroner's van and the police drove away, leaving us alone on the hot, still street.

"Come with me. I've got to close the house," he said. I went along, because the thing to do was help. Even so, I felt like one of those people who slows down at accidents on the freeway, and I wanted to run inside my home with my groceries and my dinner plans and feel the detachment I deserved.

Instead I sat in the dead widow's living room, looking for details that would help me construct her life in my mind. The room smelled like old roses. I studied the photographs of her loved ones on the end tables. That must be her son. His wife? A grandchild perhaps? And, still trying to know this woman, I noted the African violets flourishing on the window sill, the hand-crocheted doilies beneath Victorian lamps, Limoges porcelain and Lalique figures on the mantle.

Ted let Helen's little beagle in from the backyard. The dog had been looking through the glass door not making a sound. He came over to smell me, and I scooped him up on my lap being careful not to let him touch the couch. She wouldn't have liked that. His front legs stood stiff on my lap, strong and determined. He smelled like old, warm rope. I looked at the tag on his neck. Mozart.

Ted came out of the widow's bedroom holding her address book. Together we locked all the windows. As we left her house, Ted carried Mozart and I gave the geraniums a sprinkle with the hose. Then I pressed the soil around the base of each stalk to encourage the shallow roots to take hold. Walking back toward our houses, facing the end of our street with no outlet, I took Ted's hand in my soil-covered fingers and thought of my husband's tight-fitting skin.

That night at my dinner party, my husband and I toasted our guests' new house, a four-bedroom with a pool. She was expecting their first, and I attributed the new little brown spots on her hands to pregnancy. After dinner, the four of us sat outside, slapping at mosquitoes, talking until the wee hours about our hectic lives. But we kept the stereo low after 10 o'clock, that's when Ted and Velveeta turn out their lights.

SHADOWS

The gray sidewalk felt steely and frigid under the worn soles of Oscar's shoes. The cold burned his toes through damp nylon socks. He was walking away from The Cellar, where he tended bar, but not toward the subway home to Queens. He thought of his crowded two-room tenement with Anna and all those memories, and kept walking. But he wasn't going to another club, where some talkative tender would serve him a drink, straight-up. No, not tonight. He was just headed away, not toward anything, just away. He wanted to be alone, but day or night Manhattan people were always on the street, wearing their don't-mess-with-me faces, their eyes glued to the strip of cement before them.

He walked up Broadway on the curb side, watching frantic cars and cabbies, their assertive manners and near misses. He shuddered. The wind barreled down the street as through a tunnel. Oscar tightened his overcoat around his thin body. The buttons were missing so only the belt held it together, and the buckle slipped each time he took a breath. He wedged his hands in his pockets. Flecks of tobacco burrowed under his fingernails. He craved a cigarette.

"Need some company?" A woman in black fishnets and a rabbit jacket fell in step beside him.

"Got too much company," he said.

"Maybe it's just not the right kind. Anything I can do to help?"

"You wouldn't know where to begin," he muttered.

He thought about asking her for a smoke, but she was gone. Oscar walked on alone with the other restless roamers of the night. He walked three, six, ten more blocks up Broadway. Stepping and sorting thoughts, stepping, sorting. Then he ducked down a stairway to Shadows. He knew the tender there; Barry would be serving drinks all night.

"Jack Daniels?"

Oscar nodded and took the end seat at the counter.

Barry set the drink in front of him with an ashtray.

———

"You done with your stint tonight?"

"Yeah, not much of a crowd. Tips were shit."

"Same here," he said, polishing rings off the bar top as if to erase evidence of business. "How's Anna?"

"Not so good. It gets so I don't even want to go home anymore."

"She's still taking it pretty hard, huh. I can imagine. It takes a lot longer than a few weeks to get over something like that."

"Got any cigarettes?" Oscar laid a bill on the counter. Barry traded it for a pack of Salems.

In the smoke-tinted mirror behind the bar, Oscar saw how tired he looked. The outer corners of his dark eyes looked as if they had weights hanging from their red edges. Black hair fell in wilted strings over his collar. He tried to remember when he'd last had it cut, or even thought about it. He let his coat fall open. The cigarette and the drink felt warm. Glad to be on the other side of the bar, he turned to watch Barry shine the snake, straighten bottles.

Barry had a round Polish face and rear, swollen fingers, a blackjack dealer's posture and a forehead that grew beads of sweat even on the coldest days. He had a habit of wiping his forehead with his bar towel, but no one minded.

They'd met at tending school. The classes were at night, and afterward Barry would corral Oscar under

—

21

one broad arm, and in his midwestern manner, shout, "What-do-ya-say we paint the town, Charlie." (Barry called everyone Charlie.) And they'd head for a club where they'd share women and shots of tequila.

"Looks like these late nights are getting the best of you pal," Barry said. "You know we've got a day job opening here."

"Yeah, but then I'd be home nights. It's better this way."

"C'mon, lighten up. Maybe she needs you?"

"Hah, like she needs to be shot with a bazooka. She don't want nothing to do with me. Won't even speak to me. Treats me like I done the killing."

"That's just women's way, Oscar." He stood quietly for a moment, then said, "You know, there was a man in here the other night who lost his son, no, maybe it was his daughter? Anyway his kid, right?"

Oscar dropped his head and listened.

"He said he took him to a rodeo down in Texas where they were living and let him sit on the fence where they kept a bronco they was planning to break. And well the kid, I'm sure it was a son now, he fell in and the horse reared up and just planted his hoof right through the little guy's chest."

"That suppose to make me feel better?"

"Hey, I just wanted to let you know it happens. It happens to other people."

"I know already. It happened to me and I ain't got room inside right now to worry about them other people because they ain't me." He finished his drink with one bend of his wrist and laid three more bills on the counter. "Thanks for the company." He stepped through the door into the inhospitable night and headed for the subway home.

Anna was asleep as he'd hoped, or faking it. He lit a cigarette and lay on the black Naugahyde couch, which took up a third of the crowded living room. He pushed aside magazines and star-studded tabloids to make room for his feet.

Staring out the window into the emptiness, he looked past Anna's little bonsai plants hugging the window sills, clutching for whatever light they could. Their silhouettes looked like skeletons with fractured frames. Anna loved to torture those little plants with wires, impose control, keep them from becoming what they were intended.

It was nearly 4 a.m. and Oscar wondered if he would sleep. He thought about the little boy at the rodeo, if the horse got him more than once. If the man picked the boy up and covered himself in the child's blood and cursed as Oscar had done. He wouldn't have let Jesse sit on the fence. Jesse would have loved the rodeo though. He would have yelled "YeeHah" in his six-year-old voice and would have straddled a wooden bench to practice breaking that bronco himself. Oscar felt his throat thicken as if something were strangling him from the inside out. A tear built. He closed his eyes over it and slept.

Daylight broke ruthlessly into the apartment, erasing the shadows and pointing at the ashes and dust on the end tables, at the stains in the carpet, at the picture on the book case of Anna licking ice cream off Jesse's nose. Oscar woke slowly to acknowledge his pain in small doses.

He heard Anna and figured it must still be early, not yet eight o'clock. He would lie there until she left. She entered the room and Oscar could feel her watching him. He wanted to read her thoughts, to see her eyes. Hateful eyes, he was sure. He heard her leave the room and come back. She moved rarely these days, and when she did it was in slow, ponderous waves.

She was standing over him now. He wished she would bare her teeth like an animal and rip the flesh from his throat and scream "You murderer!" That would be better than her silence. Instead, starting at his feet, she gently spread a blanket over him. He her powdery perfume and the scent of cigarettes on her fingers. As her hand drew nearer his head, he reached one arm out from beneath the blanket and grabbed her wrist.

She let her hand fall limp in his grasp. Her submission seemed harsher to Oscar, crueler somehow than a struggle. At least a struggle insists there is something worth fighting.

"I thought you were asleep," she said.

"I was. Don't leave."

"I'm late." Her voice was flat.

"Anna, just spend a minute. I miss you. Talk to me."

"Not now. I'm going."

He let her flaccid wrist go, feeling foolish for having held on, and watched her leave. He heard her keys jangling softly in the pocket of her blue smock as she went slowly down the front steps. He wondered if she, too, were happier away from him and their wretched apartment.

He pulled the blanket over his head. Under the cover, buried in the smells of his stale perspiration, fetid breath and smoky clothes, he wondered whether he would ever be clean.

Although he didn't have to work until three, Oscar left the apartment before noon and, once again, canvassed the city on foot to think. He still had an hour to kill, so he walked to the Parkway Drug Store. Anna was there, the second checker from the end, smiling at the customers. He was glad she could still smile. Looking around the shabby old store with its tired linoleum and turquoise signs, which hadn't changed in the ten years Anna worked there, Oscar felt comforted that the store was much like it was the day he first went in, the day he first saw Anna.

It was summertime. Oscar had ducked into the store for the air conditioning and an ice cream. It was a year for short skirts, and when Anna bent over to scoop the ice cream, well, her legs were her best feature. Oscar asked for a double scoop.

When she handed it to him, the mint ice cream already dripping over the cone's edge, he asked, "So, do you ever get a break around here?" He remembered nervous, dryness in his mouth, the taste of socks.

"That'll be twenty-five cents," she said coolly.

"I said, do you have a break soon?" Oscar handed her a quarter.

"And if I do?"

"Well, we could take a walk. Get a soda. I don't know. What do you think?" He fumbled in his pockets, hoping he had more money.

"OK. A soda. But this isn't a date. So get that out of your mind."

He did get his date, after asking twice, and not long after learned Anna was as slippery as new leather-soled shoes. Just when he thought he'd charmed her, when she'd look in his eyes as if he were the only man in her world, she'd slip away and laugh and call him a fool and tease him in a way that made Oscar beg her to come back.

He watched her now, her quick fingers on the register. He could see the girl in the woman. She didn't have to look at the keys, sometimes she even talked with the customers while her fingers tapped away. He liked her hair long as she had it now, pulled back in simple clips. Her skin was pale and her rouge stood out under the fluorescence as if she'd put her make-up on in bad light. He slipped through the turnstyle and picked up a can of almond rocha. Her favorite. Then he got into her line.

"These are for my wife," he said before she'd had a chance to look at him.

She looked up blankly. "Will that be all?"

"Unless you have a break coming up soon."

She sighed. Oscar saw the weakening and felt hope.

"I'd like to talk," he continued. "Can't never seem to do it at home. Too much in the way I guess."

"I can only take a fifteen."

"That'll do. Coffee?"

"Sure."

They walked across the street to the coffee shop and got a table by the window.

"So, talk," she said into her cup. Her jaw was set in that way of hers, that way that said I'll be damned if I'm going to let you in.

He reached across the table for her hand. She crossed her arms. "Listen. It's hell for me, too."

She leaned back into the booth's hard orange vinyl.

"I've gone over it a thousand times, all the if onlys," he continued. "If only I hadn't decided to take Jesse to the park that day. If only we'd walked instead of taken the cab. If only I'd seen Jesse playing with the door handle. If only that cabbie coming along side of us had been five seconds later . . ."

"Stop it will you." Her voice was barely above a whisper.

"None of that wishing makes me feel a damn bit better. Nothing. None of it."

Anna wiped stripes of mascara from her cheeks with her napkin. She spoke softly in measured words as if cutting each word with a knife: "I only understand one thing, Oscar. When Jesse died I went with him."

"Anna, we can start over. It'll just take a little time, a little effort. You know what I was just doing? I was looking at apartments over in the Bronx, some with little views of Pelham Parkway. I found one sunny place, great for your plants, and it was just painted; it even smelled like a new start. And it had a dishwasher, and this old ceiling fan, built-in bookshelves. It'd be perfect."

She blotted her eyes as if trying to press the tears

---

back inside and stood up. "I've got to get back."

Oscar followed her. "At least tell me what you think."

She put on her sunglasses, brushed her hair from her temples with her fingers and said, "Sure. That would be nice."

"Anna," he said to her back. She was almost to the door. "I didn't do it."

After work that evening Oscar stopped in at Shadows. He took the end seat again. Barry was talking to two customers at the opposite end of the bar. When he saw Oscar, he brought him a Jack Daniels, setting it before him with those pudgy fingers.

"Hey, buddy," Oscar said smiling with an effort. He wanted to tell Barry that he'd found a new place on Pelham Parkway and that he and Anna were talking, but instead he lit a cigarette and said, "How are our boys doing?"

"Damn Giants. Redskins have them by the short hairs." Barry nodded toward the TV at the other end of the counter. Sports news was playing and the other men at the bar were absorbed. Barry poured himself a club soda, leaned against the cash register and took a long sip. Barry watched the TV. Oscar watched Barry.

"They get about as low as they can, though, then come back. They do something unexpected just when you've given up," Barry said without turning. "That's their way. You watch."

Oscar ran black-lined fingernails down the sides of his glass. The drink tightened his stomach, a reminder that he hadn't eaten. Because he couldn't say what was on his mind, he was quiet. He was glad Barry stayed close; even though he just stood staring at the TV not talking, that was enough. As he sat listening to Barry not talking and to the drone of the television and the distant men, he tore his napkin into four roughly even quarters. Then he pushed the small squares back into one, set his empty glass in the center to cover the seams and left.

As Oscar headed home that night, he thought about the move. He pictured Anna in the new kitchen with her plants and books around her. He'd let her pick wallpapers and decorate the bathroom in pink as she'd always wanted to. He'd work days so they could have dinners together like regular couples. Some night he'd surprise her and come home with Chinese food under one arm, a bottle of wine under the other, and they'd make love on the floor in front of their little view, their slice of the city.

When he walked into the apartment he felt happier. The place even smelled different as if the air had been shaken up. He turned on the light and called for Anna. He wanted to infect her with his plan. He went into the bedroom. She wasn't there. The bed was made.

The room felt oddly neat but changed, as if a cautious burglar had been through. Oscar felt a sickening like he did in the street that day when he held his son's body on his knees. He walked through the dark apartment calling over and over, "Anna, Anna." Just saying her name gave him hope. But the truth came forward in little stabbing signs: missing books, an empty drawer, the pictures of Jesse, gone, gone, gone.

Oscar pressed his face against the living room window where Anna's plants had been and rested his elbow heavily on the sill. The glass felt cool against his cheek. He could hear the sounds of the traffic beneath him, the shouts and cries of the lives on the street, and he watched the impatient drivers and the aimless, bustling lives. He looked down at his arm on the sill. The ledge was covered with bits of leaves and tiny pine needles. He swiped at them with his index finger then rubbed the grit into his thumb. Anna, he thought, his throat thick, she never even dusted.

THE LEGACY

March 29, 1985
From the sunny
Dear Mom,
corner of my kitchen

I'll bet you're surprised to get a letter from me. Me who always picks up the phone at any time of day without any regard to whether the phone rates are high or low. Extravagant me. See, in some ways, many ways, I'm still my mother's daughter. I'm really writing because, like you, I always sit down to read letters from loved ones. And I want you to sit down. Are you sitting? When you talk on the phone you're always involved in something else, like making banana muffins, wiping refrigerator shelves, doing your nails, especially since Pops got you that new cordless phone. Talk about extravagance. Now you can even go out into the garden and pull that nasty rye grass that creeps into the rose bed, while we chat on the phone about the last potluck you had at church, or Matilda's flea problem. (The Brewer's yeast does seem to be helping.)

Anyway, I'm writing because, are you sitting? I'm going into the hospital Monday. The mental hospital. The loony bin. I'm crazy. I know you don't know I've been seeing a shrink, but I have been for the past six months. I went in complaining of low-level depression, I figured it was because of Jerry, our rut, you know. But seems it's more than that. They suspect I've been suppressing things in my past, selective amnesia they call it, and I have to "act it out," as they say, in a "safe environment." Amazing how these things catch up with you. And I guess that's what's wrong between Jerry and me, at least that's part of it. I thought you should know because my doctor, Dr. Reynolds, Greg to us, may call you, invite you to a family session. They're big on what they call family therapy here. I told him we're not big on family therapy, but he said that was part of the problem. "Our problem" he says emphatically, yours, mine, his, so I don't blame myself so much. Doesn't really help. Anyway, don't be alarmed. I'm in good hands. Jerry's mother is taking the kids while Jerry works. I know, her house is a health hazard, but I've been instructed "not to worry." And now, I'm asking you not to worry either.

You can get up now. The worst is over. If you want to write me in the hospital, call Jerry, he'll have the address.

Love,
Suzanne

April 4, 1985

My Dear Suzanne,

What on earth is wrong! Your father and I are so concerned. For heaven's sake, Jerry told us next to nothing when we called, and he said we couldn't call you. Would our call upset you? Is it our fault? Surely your doctor must think we have a role in this, or else he wouldn't suggest we go to counseling. Your father and I are flabbergasted. But we want to warn you, be very careful with these doctors and their ideas. Don't take any drugs. Remember what happened to Aunt Lucille. All her hair turned white and she's still a mess. She was better before treatment. And remember, these doctors want to make a dollar, too. It's in their best interest to keep you in therapy, hospitalize you! It's a conflict of interest, your father says, that's business talk for they're out to make money at someone else's expense — yours in this case. I don't mean to sound alarming. I trust your ability to make decisions. And your father and I will do everything we can to be supportive. Maybe all you need is a little vacation, get away from the kids. They're a lot of work and with the remodeling going on and the way you got hit with taxes this year, no wonder you're feeling pressure, a little depressed. Have Jerry take you to Hawaii, Puerta Vallarta, you know they have many super-saver packages this time of year. You could avoid the summer rush.

I hope they let you get this in the hospital. Do they screen your mail? Really, any place that doesn't allow you phone calls. They'll probably think this is anti-hospital propaganda. That's not my intent. I'm only interested in your well-being. You know that, darling. Please write. We'd love to hear from you, although I'm sure your stay will be over quickly, and they no doubt keep you busy. (They should for what they charge. Jerry told us. That's outrageous and with no insurance for mental illness! Take the money and go to Mazatlan, I say. But you know what's best.) You're in our prayers.

Kisses and hugs,
Mom and Pops

April 10, 1985
From a smoky
lounge at Corona
Dear Mom and Pops,   Psychiatric Hospital

Thanks for the flowers and chocolates. I devoured them (the chocolates). So nice not to have little munchkins around eating up all the sweets, clutching after me with greedy hands. I also got your letter. No, they don't read my mail, they only x-ray it for sharp objects. They do look in boxes, however. But don't worry, everyone is really nice, and, like you, has my best interest in mind.

Speaking of minds, mine has been playing some funny tricks. You remember any incident with Uncle Lewis? Strange what's come up through imagery. Makes no sense, yet the anxiety that results is almost more than I can bear. (That's why the lithium. Jerry told me that upset you, but it's really helping, and it's doctor's orders. Trust me.)

Greg thinks Uncle L.'s death triggered all this. Ironic, don't you think, that he died two months before I went to see the shrink? I guess if he were around I could talk to him, but there's no point in talking to Aunt Sally. You haven't, have you? No, I don't suppose this is something you'd let out.

Anyway, I have another imagery session tomorrow. These sessions leave me frightened, disoriented and cold. I wish Pops were here to give me one of his I'll-protect-you-from-the-world hugs.

And don't worry. I'm really not as psychotic as I sound. One thing about being in a place like this, it makes your problems seem normal. You should see the woman I share a room with. She was abused in a convent and spends most of her time coloring her fingers and toe nails with purple crayon. Talk about compulsive. And her eyes are so pale that it's hard to believe they see.

My room isn't so bad. It's been newly remodeled in peach and teal after a new color study proved that particular color combination was the best for mental patients. The green in teal is supposed to incorporate nature's healing forces, while the peach stimulates healthy emotional responses. Can't hurt. The food is, well, institutional, the sheets are coarse — not 200-thread Percale — and the toilet paper is only single ply. Those are minor complaints, really, the important thing is what I'm learning. Greg says I'm a quick study and that will speed my recovery.

This weekend, I'll probably get a pass to see the kids. I'll be allowed to go to the park nearby and have a picnic. I see Jerry almost every night. Do call him, he needs some TLC.

Did your bulbs come up this year? I planted mine

---

like you said in late October, but so far no action. Maybe the California climate is different from Santa Fe's. No, that can't be, the other houses around us have blooming bulbs. I think Matilda dug them up. I found one of her bones when planting the bulbs. That must be it. Jerry and the kids say hi.

Still growing,
Suzanne

April 16, 1985

Suzanne darling,

Consider this note a hug from thirteen hundred miles away. Your mother has been pacing and long-faced since your first letter. Call her the first chance you get. Jerry tells us it will be at least another two weeks until you're discharged. Then what? Uncle Lewis was a weak man, God rest his sorry soul, please understand his weakness shouldn't be yours. Be a trouper, I know you're strong. You've got your mother's will, thank the Lord for that. Don't let those doctors brainwash you. Remember what happened to Frances in the movie. Get well soon. Jerry and the kids need you.

Here are some fruit pectins your mother and I

picked up from a fruit stand in Glover, and an article I found on raising quail. I remember you talked about that once. Be well.

All my love,
Pops

April 22, 1985

Dear Mom and Pops,

No time or desire to write today. So I'll just send this clip from my journal. Maybe you'll understand. See a light that I can't:

Sometimes I wish I could detach myself like this woman who shares my room can. Her eyes and skin are so light and mine are so black, like my insides. And beneath my dark shell the core of my body seems to spin relentlessly, with an invincible gravity pulling me down, begging me to give in, to give up. Sometimes I walk into the room in my mind and see only a box and I open the box to find it's Uncle Lewis's coffin or Mom's face, alive and laughing. My mind is opening painful new corridors, and I'm seeing things I never dreamed were possible.

Suzanne

Dear Suzanne,

What are they doing to you, darling? You don't sound like yourself at all. If you were still under our care, I'd have you taken out of there immediately, but Jerry won't hear of it. Someone has convinced him this is good for you. Your father has started smoking again. You know how worried he must be. Our lives are in utter turmoil. We haven't been to the club in weeks, or even out for that matter. We can't bear to speak to anyone of this. As for this imaging business, remember the mind is a powerful organ. It can play tricks on you, deceive you.

As you suspected, Greg called. We had a nice long chat. He sounds like a competent and sympathetic fellow, but I'm still leery of his methods. He asked us a lot of questions. Of course, we were as helpful as we could be, but have you ever thought of telling him that this is plain none of his business? Your father said as much, but I hastened to add that we'd be glad to cooperate in any way we can. Whatever it takes, really. Just as soon as Pops can get away from work, we'll fly out in a jiffy. We'll help you once you're home. And when will that be? Goodness, it's been four weeks now. I simply can't believe they keep you in a locked ward and don't even allow your own children to visit.

That's utterly inhumane. Be careful darling. Everything will be just fine.

Chin up,
Mom

P.S. Our garden is lovely. Snap dragons are blooming, and the irises and ranunculus came up right on schedule. Matilda, that rascal.

May 2, 1985

Mom,

    You're wondering how long I have to stay and I'm asking how long until I have to leave. I've grown rather fond of this locked-up world. Sometimes I think I never want to leave to face my life. The truth, a puzzle, is becoming painfully clear. I'm remembering things now, just bits of things, I couldn't possibly imagine. These memories are real scenes, with real words spoken by real people. I remember Uncle Lewis coming in Aunt Sally's sewing room. You'd left me there, and Aunt Sally stepped out, leaving me alone with Uncle Lewis, and I was terrified, apparently this wasn't the first time. His red, rash-like skin seemed redder, blotchier, and I shuddered at the horror of its touch. His leer I could avoid, because I closed my eyes. But not his touch, nor his smell, although I tried at the time not to breathe. I felt trapped, and I moved against the wall, wrapping myself in a piece of flowered voile that Aunt Sally had been sewing on. I wrapped it tightly around my flat chest in meek protection and curled up onto the floor with my eyes closed. Still, when I close my eyes, I can hear Uncle Lewis. He was saying, is saying, in a raised voice, because I had my hand over my ears. "You're just like your mother, you sweet little frightened thing, and I'm going to have you, your mother, you, your mother, sweet thing."

I hadn't remembered this until now, Greg says, because I was protecting myself, coping. Surviving. Only now I don't want to cope or survive. But I don't have the will to give up. I've written letters to the children. Someday they'll have to know the truth, too. But first, there's more to know; I have to have the answers. And I must get rid of these voices.

Still searching,
Suzanne

May 6, 1985

Dear Jerry,

We can't get through to her anymore. They're killing her, and she's letting them, all because of these preposterous mind games and those drugs they've got her on. And now she's hallucinating, inventing these horrible scenes, talking about dying and letters to the children. Don't you see that she was happier before any of this. What good could they be doing? Please help her, we know she loves you so, and the kids, think of the poor children. You're in our prayers continually.

Love,
Becky and Sid

May 8, 1985

Dear Dr. Greg Reynolds:

How can you call yourself a mental health professional, when you've thrown our daughter into suicidal jeopardy? This lunacy is your doing. My wife and I have written a letter to the psychiatric board of medical examiners urging that your license be revoked. Anyone who stirs up such dangerous hallucinations that have no basis in fact and serve only to destroy families and lives ought to be himself locked up, permanently. Once our daughter is free of your insidious institution, we'll insist she not return. We'll be a lifetime repairing your damage.

Willfully,
Mr. and Mrs.
Sidney Albrecht

—

Mom,

The hardest truths, I now know, take the longest to surface. The pain is unimaginable, but at least I can begin to heal. My worries now are for you. How have you lived with this? Uncle Lewis told me everything, to punish you in his deranged way. He made me promise, with threats, that I would never tell, never even hint that I knew you and he were lovers.

The night is so vivid to me now. I can't understand how I could have put it away. You and Uncle Lewis laughing in the front bedroom, beneath an open window, him on top, your screams then your laughter. I remember your face when you saw me standing in the door, your surprise when you saw I was witness. I remember standing there in a blue nightie that left my ankles bare; my feet, like my insides, were as cold as the glass of that bedroom window. Don't you remember? Or did you suppress it, too? And you told me it was just a bad dream.

But the bad dream came later, the past 25 years, as I dreamt all along, deluding myself, pretending along with you, the Albrechts are such a nice family. After you cut him off, he started with me to get even with you, maybe to somehow replace you. It all makes sense now, in a perverse way.

Get away, you say, escape (deny). But now I know better. I know you better. I'm the one who's really gotten away. And that's the good news. I'm free now. Sure I still feel compelled to punish myself. But that I can work through. I can't forgive you yet, but you have my sympathy. I'll be home soon, sooner than I'd like, no doubt. Don't bother coming out. I'll be just fine.

Stronger,

Suzanne

June 10, 1985

Dear Suzanne, Jerry, Holly, Peter and Matilda:

The picture on this post card is of the beach in Rio. Our hotel is right on the sand. Pops and I are having a wonderful time. It's such a colorful city, and hot. We'll send lots of goodies. I'm so glad, Suzanne, you're home and well. I'm also glad you started this business of writing letters. You're right, in many ways it's better than the phone, much better.

Kisses and bear hugs,

Grandma and Pops

PEACE TIME

On a windy hilltop campus of a farmland university there is a small slice of a man. A tan man who sits on the edge of a brick planter every day there's no rain or snow. He never speaks. He never smiles. But he sometimes stands with his arms crossed, letting the warm sun spread across his bare skin and the wind dance with his straight locks of brown sunstreaked hair. And he always wears faded blue corduroy shorts, the ribbing long worn off in two equal circles over his rear. No shirt. No shoes.

Only new students question his presence. Then soon they, too, begin to worry where he sleeps at night and where he spends the winter. Otherwise his being there is as much a part of the campus as the steam whistle that blows every 15 minutes past the hour, loosing the students from their classes in teeming rivers.

He came out of Nam that way, they say. Shell shock. And the students, virile young sons and their lovers, cherish the campus crucifix, knowing, not fully, how grateful they are to be a generation without war. Even still they march in front of the union. Kill Khomeini, they chant. They don't quite see their young lives as gambling chips — black, red, green, what value?

Every morning before the protests begin and just as the university newspaper is hitting the stands, the tan man arrives riding a rusty blue bike with a bell but no basket. He parks in the rack alongside the students' bikes, always the same slot, the far one on the right. Then he takes his brick perch. First lying stomach down, like a desert snake, to warm his dark, leathery, sun-spotted back. Then he stands, a fractured posture, watching the students, or the sky, or the robins and squirrels fighting in the trees. And sometimes he sits with his knees drawn up like a monkey's, looking out through a weather-aged face with eyes that grow emptier. When the sun disappears and the students are gone, he gets his blue bike and disappears over the hilltop.

One yellow day heavy with spring, the tan man

---

didn't come. No one paid much attention at first. Then after a week, when the silent pressure of his absence had swollen to the point of disturbance, the university paper sent out its best reporters who, although they couldn't find out where he lived, or slept, or ate, discovered that a tan man had suddenly appeared on a university campus a few states away, a campus also known for its unrest. A quiet concern grew among the students. And out of what seemed to be an unspoken consensus, no one sat in the tan man's place, and his bike slot was left vacant, as if in a respectful effort to preserve his peaceful presence.

Eventually, the emptiness prompted the paper to create a campaign to get the tan man back, running a series of editorials in the opposing school's paper. There had never been so much talk of the tan man. Some students even sent letters to him, knowing they could no more reach him than if they stood before him. Meanwhile, the campus protests mounted, and, as if in response, a new cause emerged. Students posted hand-bills displaying the tan man above the slogan, "World Peace at What Cost?"

Gradually, the unrequited effort to get the tan man back waned, and the students consumed themselves with other concerns — a new theatre for the drama department, the impeachment of a tenured professor.

Summer emptied the classrooms and hallways,

---

and in the fall freshman sat on the brick wall and placed their bikes in the once-reserved stall. Slowly the tan man's lingering spirit faded, then disappeared with the finality of winter.

Bright red tulips in front of the new drama theatre and daffodils in the brick planter greeted the students after the cold months. Then one day, not long after the thaw, the tan man in his corduroy shorts walked up the hillside, pushing his rusty bike. He leaned his bike against the brick wall and sat near his old place, beside two students who eyed him critically then left. In front of the Union the marchers continued their hollow chant: US out of El Salvador. And the hari krishnas in orange robes talked of peace and chimed finger bells. And the tan man tucked his knees up under his chin, wrapped his arms around them and rocked himself, swaying rhythmically to some internal tune.

FACADE

So call it a weak moment. A lapse. Temporary insanity. We all have those moments, no? Times when we think eating a jumbo Hershey's bar will make us feel better, or not speaking to our mother will make her get the message. Crazy, right? Well it happens.

I was feeling far too old at twenty-six to be starting an acting career. I should have started as a teen porn star like all those women my age who had already made it, but I didn't have the breasts. Instead I was busy in college preparing for my future, studying computer science, trying to learn to make "intelligent" decisions.

So on the day of the lapse, I was aware that as far as my new career was concerned I was too late, practically as far gone as the tyrannosaurus. I was feeling, well, *insecure*. That's how I wound up in that make-up department in South Coast Plaza, where Southern California's beautiful people shop and dine.

Now I had no business in this upscale shopping center. My husband Alex and I had agreed that if I gave up my computer job to do this acting thing I wasn't going to be able to have my shopping binges too. He was all behind my pursuing a new career, developing my talents, but we'd have to cut back, live off one income, *sacrifice*. That means no charges, he'd said. If we can't pay cash, we don't buy.

So I started to think about what innocuous purchase I could make. Alex never quibbled if I bought new lace lingerie, so I started in the foundations department of Bullock's, toying with the idea of falsies. That took all of 20 minutes. But it was long enough for me to notice, beneath those merciless fluorescent lights, how pale I looked.

So I headed downstairs to the make-up counter that featured a line of exclusive French cosmetics and began dabbling in the blush samples: Pomme Vivant, Pêche et Crème, Vin Rosé. The names sounded capable of transformations. I noticed a perfectly made up, unblemished saleswoman watching me as I drew on my cheeks in the oval mirror. She was wearing a crisp mint-green smock that made her look clean, exact and clinical. I imagined she smelled like Pinesol, but as she approached I smelled camellias. Her brown hair was tied back with a neat green bow.

"Is eye puffiness always a problem for you?" she whispered confidentially.

"Why, yes, I guess it is," I confessed.

"I mean if you'd been crying or something, I could understand, but if that's not the case. What do you use on your face?"

Now this was embarrassing. "Just Pond's cold cream and baby oil to take off my eye make-up."

"That's it," she said. Her pony tail bobbed with assertion. "All that oil and heavy cream seeps right down in through your tear ducts and gets trapped right in here." She took one of her carefully polished, scarlet nails and traced the pouch beneath my right eye.

Then she took the back of her finger and ran it along the side of my face. "And your skin is *so* dehydrated. What do you moisturize with?"

I was devastated. How could I have been so negligent? Then she mentioned the layer of dead skin cells on my face. That was the clincher. I couldn't leave the counter and go out among the beautiful people of South Coast Plaza let alone go on camera with a face that looked like the floor of Death Valley.

The woman took me firmly by the arm to her

———

stool. "Sit here," she said. Soon another green smock came out to assist. This one had a full bouffant of henna-red hair that looked as if the men were still inside working on it, and freshly glossed lips outlined painstakingly in crimson to suggest curves that didn't exist.

Just in case I wasn't already convinced of the deplorable condition of my ailing epidermis, the first green smock held a device to my face that projected my skin, 10 times magnified, onto a closed-circuit television. That was bad enough, but then I realized the monitor was hooked up to several other monitors throughout the make-up area. My God! There it was, bigger than life, my poor, flaking, parched, spotty skin, exposed, crying to be hidden, giving new meaning to the word natural, and leaving me inside it wishing vainly for an out-of-body experience.

Passersby stopped and stared in disbelief at the screens, as the smocks, among the crowd's gasps, pointed out the fine texture changes, dead cells, pigment irregularities. Two middle-aged women kept staring at the screen, then at me, then at the screen, whispering between themselves and clutching their chins in horror. Good Lord, the smocks agreed, we had to act fast.

And so they began, cleansing, massaging, masking, exfoliating, peeling, toning, moisturizing. All the while they spoke to each other in soft, concerned tones. Their little phrases buzzed in my mind: "impending facial lines . . . now was the time to start . . . dry skin . . . those dirty old tenacious dead cells . . . Pond's! . . . Can you imagine? . . . Baby oil!" I was lucky to be finding this out now and not a moment later, the first green smock told me. How old did I say I was?

"Thirty," I lied.

The smocks worked with concentration on my face. The second green smock fetched and carried product after product to the first green smock who applied them. New sensations — tingly, crackly, gooey, cool — accompanied each application. The eye-make-up remover was guaranteed to prevent puffiness, while the cool aqua gel mask was designed to draw the puffiness out of the eyes, leaving them "taut and toned." There were four moisturizers alone. One for the eyes, one for the rest of the face, except the jawline, which had its own moisturizer, which was different from the moisturizer for the throat and neck. (They assured me the most noticeable signs of age were the choker like circles around a woman's neck.) And these four moisturizers, of course, didn't include the night creams, which they promised to explain.

How could one ever keep track? I asked. Do people really do this every day? Oh, yes, they assured me. It

———

becomes habit. Like brushing your teeth. And to help me form the habit they were going to write down every product in the order I was to use it in two columns — a.m. and p.m.

Simple. No sweat.

After they finished stripping and steaming and cleaning and saturating, they handed me a mirror. The first green smock said. "There now doesn't your skin look better?" Her pony tail bobbed in agreement. The second green smock smiled. I watched the line around her lips expand and contract.

Every blood vessel in my face was at attention, every freckle proud, my naked eyes, the eyes that only my bathroom mirror sees, looked terrified. "You're not going to let me leave like this," I said.

That's when the second green smock took over. "She's our make-up expert," said the first green smock. Quickly, green smock two covered my face with concealer to cover the blotches and freckles. That was followed by foundation with sunscreen, so I wouldn't get more blotches and freckles. Then came the blush, at last. For a moment I'd forgotten what I'd come for.

"I'd like a slightly darker blush than the shade I was wearing, to emphasize my cheekbones," I said.

"Oh certainly, but really you need two. You should wear Prune Panache here and Raisin Fumé here, for drama."

"But of course."

"And when you get to the eyeliner, I like black."

"Certainly, but mixed with midnight blue. Blue will help make your tired eyes look whiter," she said with a whisper.

And so she continued blushing and brushing, painting and dabbling in various palates and tubes of color, occasionally consulting with the first green smock, who was busy writing down every product in its order and its method and place of application. The first shade of blush should not be applied too low on the cheek. Eye shadow should be — never horizontal, horizontal was out — blended in vertical lines, slate then yellow (for contrast with my blue eyes), then mauve. And the eye pencil should never extend across the entire lid. No, no, no, it should stop mid-way.

"I never would have thought of that," I kept saying.

The first green smock was a marvelous audience. Raving about every color selection, as if with each application I was transforming before her eyes into Aphrodite. "What fabulous coverage. You do great eyes. That yellow is a sheer stroke of genius." I was beginning to feel radiant.

Then the touche finale. Green smock two took a fine brush and stroked it gently down my face in only one direction. I lifted my eyebrows in a way that asked

"Now what are you doing?"

Straightening your facial hairs," she said. "They should all go in one direction."

"My facial hairs? I've never thought about which way facial hairs go." No wonder I can't make it in acting, I thought. Crooked facial hairs are probably the equivalent of yellow teeth or pock-marked skin in this business.

"A technicality," she said, "but an important one."

Green smock one added a face brush to the list.

I consulted the mirror while the two smocks pulled together all the products I *had* to have. I did look a good deal better than usual, I had to admit. My skin was hydrated, free of those cruddy skin cells. My face felt smooth, rejuvenated. And green smock two did have a way with color. But, I would exercise prudence. "Just give me the basics today," I said firmly, "I can always come back for the rest."

"Well you need this," began smock number one, picking up a slick, chrome-coated box and putting it on the counter in a "must" pile, "to cleanse the face every morning. And the toner is also a must."

"And you need this to restore the moisture balance in your skin," said green smock two, adding to the pile, "and this to fend off skin cells, and this . . ."

I heard Alex's voice: "Sacrifice."

"No, leave out the jaw cream and the throat cream.

———

I'll have to make the face cream stretch. And leave off the peel mask.''

Then I heard the first words of green smock one: "Is eye puffiness always a problem for you?''

"But I'll take that gel that reduces eye puffiness and your make-up remover that won't clog my ducts.''

My husband's voice intrudes: "I'm behind you, darling, but we'll have to cut back, no shopping binges.''

"But keep the mascara, the foundation and the concealer. I have all that. I'll just take one blush, the darker one. And only two of those four eye shadows, the yellow one and whatever other one you think.''

As green smock one started adding up my bare-minimum purchase, a woman announced over the loudspeaker that the store would be closing in five minutes. I looked at my watch. 9:30! I'd been in the chair more than two hours! No wonder I'd never looked better. Who has *that* kind of time to put make-up on every day? My heart pounded. I hadn't asked the price of anything. I counted out 12 boxes in my purchase, optimistically I tallied $12 a piece, $150 total, max. Still the thought of spending that on cosmetics seemed preposterous, yet so necessary. It could mean my career, my edge on the competition.

"Will this be cash or charge?'' It was green smock one.

I heard my husband's voice: "That means no charges."

I handed her my Bullock's card.

She handed me the bill, pointing with her neat red fingernail at the grey X for my signature. Her palm covered the bottom line. I slid the bill out from beneath her hand to pull the total into view. My stomach felt like it did the time the youth pastor caught me drinking whiskey at church camp. My cheeks grew even redder. I slid the bill back under her palm and signed. $289. Green smock two was wrapping each product in tissue and filling a large shopping bag.

Finally, I mustered my courage and said, "Do you suppose there are any duplicate products here, I mean something we can eliminate?"

The two smocks looked at each other, then green smock two said, "We don't sell duplicate products."

"No, of course not, how silly."

When I got home that night I wanted to show Alex my cheekbones, but he was in bed. I quietly put away the goods, hiding the bag and receipt. I took out the instructions titled "p.m." Four steps: cleanser, toner, eye-make-up remover, night cream. Aqua gel mask optional. I applied it all — even the mask for puffiness — in the proper sequence. Once freshly scrubbed and moisturized I slid luxuriously and guiltily into bed.

———

I was sure when Alex saw my radiant skin, I'd be able to justify my purchase, at least in part. But the next morning, as he leaned over to greet me in bed, the first thing he said was, "What happened to your eyes?" He didn't even have his glasses on.

"What? What's wrong with my eyes?"

"Honey, you've got to get to a doctor. They're all swollen, like you have an allergy."

"I'll kill them." I headed for the mirror. Sure enough the bags beneath my eyes hung like reddened half moons. And the upper lids were thickened and inflamed. "It must be that new eye make-up remover I picked up yesterday," I said lightly.

I spent the morning lying down applying alternately cucumber slices and iced cloths to my eyes. An agency called and asked if I could make an audition that afternoon. I'd see, I said. I called back later and said I was sorry, I had other business.

By afternoon the swelling had gone down, but the redness remained. I took the products and put them all back in the bag with the receipt. Then I took out a few and put them in what I thought of as a maybe bag. And, wearing a pair of dark glasses, I headed for Bullock's. Behind the make-up counter stood a different green smock. This lady was older, well-preserved, and sanitary. When she smiled the scars from her face lift stood out in front of her ears. I explained my plight, took off my glasses, laid it on thick about the eye puffiness story, handed her my purchase and receipt, and asked for a credit.

"I simply can't tolerate your products," I said in summary.

"But all our cosmetics are hypo-allergenic, what you need is this." And she showed me a blue liquid in a bottle. "You apply this after your eye make-up remover and aqua gel mask to strip away any remaining chemicals. I assure you, use this and you won't have any more trouble."

"Are you crazy?" I asked.

She wasn't, she said.

"This is insane. This is ragtime. I don't need any of this," I said. "I'm a struggling actress and I already missed an audition today because of your eye experiments." Customers were beginning to stop and watch.

"Would you like to speak to the manager?" She said as coolly as if her mint-green smock were refrigerated.

I was enjoying the stage. I never realized how much I liked being a spectacle. So maybe acting was my calling. "No, you'll do just fine. As long as you'll take these miserable, over-priced things back and credit my account. I won't be a dupe for any more of your products or your hype."

I began unloading products one by one on the counter. "It's back to baby oil and Pond's for me. They never gave me any trouble and they're a heck of a lot cheaper." I slapped each product loudly on the counter for emphasis. The crowd that had gathered was riveted. The first bag was empty. Then I got to the second bag. My pace slowed a bit. I returned the toner, the face cream and the facial brush. Then I started to take out the exfoliating cream, but I thought of those dead skin cells and weakened. I dropped it back into the maybe bag, which became the yes bag. And there it stayed alongside the yellow eye shadow, which really did give my eyes contrast, and with the blush. I needed the blush.

SUMMER SCHOOL

"I just can't imagine a girl of her, well, *stature* going out with a boy and not wearing a bra." Mom was talking to Dad about Larry's date.

"Oh Fran let them be. Just be glad he's dating, finally. Dating *girls*." Larry was sixteen — old enough to drive, grow sideburns and use bad words with authority. I was younger by three years and eager to catch up.

"At least he wore clean jeans, Mom," I contributed, but she didn't seem to hear. She had worked herself into a dither.

It was the first time Larry had abandoned his electric guitar on a Friday night, and he did it to take out a

———

buxom girl with freckles who looked as if she'd come from a farm. But she didn't. She came from Costa Mesa like the rest of us.

Frankly, I didn't know what he saw in her. She never dressed for P.E. (Always said she had cramps.) She swayed when she walked — and would not be hurried; her idea of a smile was a smirk, and she never opened her eyes all the way. Although we didn't have much use for her, Stephanie, my best friend in those days, and I were grateful for Christine this particular night, because now we had something to look forward to.

The year was 1973. It was summer, July, and hot.

Because Steph and I were restless and eager to move on with things, on slow nights we went to "summer school." That was our code name, or what we called this hobby of ours — sneaking around the neighborhood, peering in windows, catching snatches of conversation and life. We didn't know there were words for this sort of behavior: "eavesdropping," "voyeurism." But we liked it just the same. It gave us an electric feeling in our bladders.

And sure enough, after the movie, Larry took Christine back to his bedroom.

There had been some discussion of this before Larry left. "If I bring her back here," Larry was making clear, "I want to be left alone, or I'll find somewhere else to go." He was figuring on Mom's offering tea and brownies at exactly the wrong moment.

"Honestly, you'd think we didn't have any consideration for your privacy." Mom addressed us kids with the same Christian tolerance she exercised on her first grade class. She looked to Dad for help. Her prim blue dress didn't mask the fact she was rattled.

Steph and I sat on the floor of the family room playing hearts, pretending not to listen.

"You go right ahead and bring your friend home. We'll stay out of your way, son. But understand this is a privilege. Don't blow it." Dad always sounded funny when he tried to use hip phrases. He was an engineer, a no-nonsense, bottom-line guy. His white shirt had a blue-ink-stained pocket despite the plastic pocket sleeve Mom insisted he wear.

When he finished talking, he didn't look at Mom, who couldn't hide her disappointment. She worried a line between her brows, which threatened at her age to be permanent. Larry sauntered out. He tossed the car keys once into the air — probably for our benefit — then crammed them in his front pocket.

After he left my parents kept talking, still as if Steph and I weren't there:

"Well I'd rather have him home than parked somewhere and caught in some unlawful and compromising position," Dad said, trying to reassure Mom.

"But we have a responsibility to, to her parents."
Mom was more educated than Dad and more naive.
(Like, she believed my brother once when he came
back from a ski trip and told her the purple mark on his
neck was from a snow ball. When Larry came up with
that explanation, Dad looked across the room at me
and winked. I remember how smug I felt knowing
more than my mother, being privy to a secret.)

"For Pete's sake, Fran, the boy's palms were
sweating before he left. Nothing's going to happen. Be
glad he *wants* to come home."

Steph shuffled the cards so half the deck faced the
wrong way. I could tell she didn't want to play anymore. I'd won the last three games. Her cheeks were
bright pink in spots and peeling. Zinc oxide, left over
from a day at the beach, outlined the rough spots on
her nose.

I motioned to her with my head and we moved to
the backyard. We sat on the lawn beside a small group-
ing of yuccas and a sego palm. We stretched our legs
out and automatically compared tans. I took a long
piece of grass and started trailing it up the inside of my
leg, stopping just below the fringe of my cut-offs. And I
felt the pressure, like a bubble just under my sternum.

We didn't know this then, in fact the lesson was
just beginning, that the pressure rises and falls but
never goes away, that it lingers everywhere, behind

every knee, in the small of every back, in the breath and pores of every person in a checkout line, in a current that runs between people on the sidewalk.

Steph leaned back on her arms to watch the seagulls float, lift, dive.

I learned then and since then — this has taken some time — that growing up in Southern California is different. Perhaps it's because of the permissive climate, the beach, the fertile soil, and the fact that people are comfortable wearing almost nothing. For kids coming of age in Southern California, learning has little to do with school and everything to do with living.

That year, for all those years, my family lived in a California tract home, close enough to the beach to smell it but too far from it to walk. That night the air was warm and damply thick with salt. Larry's bedroom burned with black-light posters and incense. Mom referred to his room loudly and often as the den of iniquity. He and Christine must have been boiling in there with that incense smoking and the door nearly shut.

The air outside was beginning to cool but still no breeze. Even in the dark, the bricks beneath my brother's bedroom window retained the day's heat. That's where Steph and I knelt, crouched low against the brick planter, peering through azalea blossoms, hoping my brother would make a move.

But Christine and Larry just sat there, on the carpet, leaning against the side of twin beds, facing each other. Christine's t-shirt glowed white under the black light. Neither of them was talking. In fact neither was doing anything. Just sitting. Posters of Jimi Hendrix and John Lennon radiated down from the ceiling. Led Zeppelin was cranked up so loudly on the stereo that I could feel the music vibrate where my chest pressed the bricks.

"Let's go. I want to go," Steph whispered. "This is boring."

"Shhh. Just wait a minute."

We stayed watching for a while longer.

"Nothing's going to happen," she said.

"Wait." I squeezed her upper arm to make her look.

They'd both kicked off their sandals, and my brother started rubbing his feet against hers. Then he ran the side of his toe up the side of her leg, inside her bell-bottom jeans. He kept this up for some time.

"So they're playing footsies. Big deal. They're not even talking. Boy, is she a dud." Steph had turned from the window and was leaning with her back against the bricks.

The fact that they seemed to be getting along fine not talking is what interested me. And I kept watching. Their toes made slow, careful circles around each other's feet. First his foot slid over and under each of hers. Then hers over and under his. The turntable spun. Robert Plant sang "Ocean."

We sat there until we heard the Disneyland fireworks start. Because you could see the fireworks from Larry's room, we thought he and Christine might come to the window. So we moved out in a hurry, never thinking that they couldn't possibly hear the fireworks over the stereo or the sound of their skin.

As it turned out, that was one of our more memorable nights in summer school. Today, fifteen years later, every time I hear a twig snap by the window or think I hear the sound of denim scraping against the stucco outside, I imagine I'm being watched. Serves me right. As a result, I live my life as if some impressionable youth were watching my every move, as if I were making an imprint on his mind.

"I don't think we should," Stephanie said when we had our first summer-school experience. "What if she sees us."

The first time was by accident. It was dusk, and we were sitting outside the Lawrences' house on the curb with our feet in the gutter. They lived at the bottom of the street, and the sprinkler water that ran down from all the houses above pooled outside their place, making the deepest, coolest spot for feet soaking.

From the curb we heard Julie Lawrence in the

71

bathroom. Actually, we heard the transistor radio she'd brought into the bathroom. We were intrigued with Julie, who had been away at college and was home for the summer, and we watched her every chance we got.

"Come on," I whispered.

Steph seemed a little nervous, but followed me to the edge of the bathroom windowsill. Good thing the radio was on because we hadn't yet learned to be quiet. Julie was sitting without a top on, wearing a yogurt mask on her face. At least we figured it was yogurt because the empty Knudsen's container sat on the sink. She was positioning a pencil horizontally under the fold of one breast. Then she stood. The pencil fell with a clack. Then she did the same to the right breast. When she stood the pencil stayed. She repeated the process several times, referring to a magazine that lay open beside her. Sometimes the pencil would fall and sometimes it wouldn't.

"What's she doing?" Steph asked.

"Be quiet," I said because I didn't know.

"Think she's weird?"

"Maybe a little."

Nevertheless, we both went straight back to my house and tried the same thing.

"You don't have to try it, you already know what will happen," Steph said with her shirt off. She was developing a bit faster than I and somehow I was more embarrassed. I didn't know until I was well into high school that at 13, according to some magazine, both Steph and I could afford to go braless.

So that's how this summer school thing started. Like I said, by accident. Soon, however, we couldn't help ourselves. We had to fuel this constant feeling, which felt kind of like a hum, that we were always on the edge of something exciting. Every evening, before twilight, Steph and I would sit out front eating sunflower seeds and drinking Diet Pepsi watching who was going out for the evening. Like burglars, we studied the layout of each house, the habits of each household. We'd wait for backyard barbecues to move indoors and lights in various rooms to come on and stay burning. We had a rule never to go to a window in a house until the light had been on at least five minutes, long enough for the person to get in and settled.

We planned a circuit: The Lotts, the Seymours, the Fastiggis, sometimes the Downings. (The Downings' house was where we had our closest call. One night, Mr. Downing — he was young enough so that we called him Pete — was away, and we were hiding among the garbage pails watching his wife, Jill, and she wasn't fat yet, in her bedroom consume an entire — and I mean entire — half gallon of ice cream while she read *Lady Chatterley's Lover.* I guess she didn't want the reminder of her gluttony in the kitchen trash, so she came out to throw the container in the outside garbage. The pail she hit was right next to Steph's head. It was close, but she didn't turn on the light and we both knew to wear dark clothes.)

The Lawrences' house and the Seymours' were the best because they only had neighbors on one side and they kept their bathroom windows partly open. All the other bathroom windows on the block were closed and had that opaque glass. This we knew, as we knew who kept their barking dogs outside, who had bushes that rustled, leaves that crunched and gates that creaked. (These had to be jumped.) We liked bathrooms and bedrooms best, but if nights were slow, dens and family rooms would do.

After the fireworks, after we left Larry and Christine, we headed for the Seymours' because the Lawrences' were clearly not home. Mrs. Seymour was inclined to walk around in her negligée. Mr. Seymour never seemed to notice and spent long sessions in the bathroom reading *Penthouse* on the john. They could afford this laxness because their kids were grown and gone. The thing to remember about the Seymours was that their automatic sprinklers went on at 10:30 p.m.

This night, they were watching TV in bed. We could tell by the movement of light and shadow coming from their room, and the pitched voices and tinny music whining through their open bedroom window.

———

The bedroom side of their house was easy. No noisy foliage to betray us. Just a soft quiet lawn and a retaining wall that acted as a step, our perch to the window of their bedroom. After only a minute even the crickets accepted us and started chirping again.

They sat on their bed, backs to the window. We looked down through the dim light over Mr. Seymour's balding head, Mrs. Seymour's dull, once-red hair. She wore a pale waltz-length nightie and extended her legs over the bed covers. The only light in the room came from the television.

We ducked as Mr. Seymour got up to turn the channel to "Hawaii Five-O," then slowly raised our heads to peer over the lip of the window after he settled back on on the bed and lit a cigarette. He burped as if he were alone, not bothering to cover his mouth. Mrs. Seymour seemed not to notice him at all. He stared at the television and breathed so we could hear it. His bare stomach pushed out over his shorts. I wondered how, with that stomach and his heavy, stale breath, and Mrs. Seymour's stiff bouffant, how they ever did it.

A commercial for pantyhose came on. A smart-looking tall woman walked down a street, turning men's heads. Mrs. Seymour went into the bathroom. She took one of those hand-held massagers that have the little plastic rolling balls in the hand piece and started rolling the back of her neck.

———

"Why doesn't anyone ever do anything?" Steph asked as we left the Seymours'. She had a way of asking the very thing I was thinking, then I'd have to answer. We were both disappointed in the Seymours.

"Like what?" I stalled.

"Don't be stupid."

We walked back toward my house under a dark moonless sky that made the hour seem later than it was. The air was considerably cooler, damp and briny. The street was quiet except for a group of older kids who sat on the corner smoking. Some sat on the curb, some sat on laps and some on cruiser bikes, probably ripped off from Mesa Beach Rental. They wore drawstring pants and hooded sweat jackets. Their sunbleached hair shone beneath street lamps. The cherries from the cigarettes they passed glowed thick and hot and bobbed in the grey, smoky, moist, lamp-lit air.

As we got closer to the house, we heard "Smoke on the Water" playing and remembered my brother and Christine. This time Steph lead the way, and quietly we knelt by the brick planter. The bedroom window was open wider, to cool the room off no doubt. And the bedroom door was open more than a crack, probably at my mother's insistence. My brother and Christine lay in the center of the room between the two twin beds, one black-lit form. A swirl of musky denim. He was over her, his leg hooked around hers, linked at the knee, and they were rocking, gently rock-ing.

The last song on the album ended. The record spun quietly to a stop, so then we could hear the long, soft pah-pah of their breath, and the sound of rubbing — denim against denim, denim against skin, skin against skin. We crouched by the planter, as quiet as fog, straining to see through the screen and the dark, incense-filled room to the figures inside. Stephanie didn't blink, and I knew she was wondering as I was what it must be like.

THE GAS STATION

When the bell rang on the full-service island, Danny, taking but a second longer than usual, hung up the phone and ran out to help a man pacing beside a Mercedes. He wore an overcoat and sucked long draws from his cigarette.

"Fill it?"

The man answered with a sharp downward jerk of his chin.

Danny held a blue rag beneath the nozzle he placed in the tank. He washed each window and wiped up the thin trails of water that streamed from his squee-gee before they reached the paint. He got back to the nozzle before it popped out so he could top off the tank

---

without spilling.

"That's $23.87."

The man flipped him a plastic card, then taking the rag wiped a toe print from his rear bumper. He got back in his car. Danny handed him the draft. He signed it aggressively, helped himself to his copy and handed the rest back to Danny. As the man started to raise his tinted power window, Danny said, "Merry Christmas," but wished he hadn't.

Before the window completely closed, however, Danny thought he heard the man say, "You, too."

Danny Garrison was a C-minus student with bad skin and a red stubble of a beard where his razor couldn't reach. He wore optimistically tight pants that didn't suit him and around his neck, a silver Saint Christopher on a chain. The gas station where he worked was on a busy corner, one of the busiest in the San Fernando Valley. Here, hurried customers displaced their frustrations on the attendants. Whether Danny noticed or cared didn't matter. He was used to it.

After the Mercedes left, Danny walked back toward the garage. Mike was there fixing a tire for a lady. She was the kind of lady who made Danny want to wash his hands and clean up the place. He'd seen her in the station before. She drove a white Peugeot, usually went to self serve and wore sunglasses even when it

—

was overcast and cold. The radio played Christmas carols. A well-known male voice was singing "Here Comes Santa Claus."

"That was my dad on the phone," Danny said.

"So what do you want, a medal?" Mike was trying to impress the lady.

"That must be a pretty slow leak," the lady said. "Can you find it?" Mike was studying the treads.

"I'll find it."

"I'm going to see him tonight," said Danny.

"Yeah, so? Don't worry, we'll find this sucker." Mike moved to a faucet outside the garage and began filling a tub. The lady and Danny followed him. The lady stared at the dragon tattoo on Mike's forearm. "All I have to show for Nam," he'd told Danny once, as he singed the hairs that covered it with a match.

"So I've never seen him, that's what."

Danny noticed the lady's eyebrows raise a little behind her dark glasses, but she kept her eyes on the tire.

"He took one look at you and left," Mike said and chuckled. "Can you blame him? How's our gas level?"

"We're running out. We've only got about four inches."

"Look!" said the lady, pointing to the tire.

"Ahh," said Mike who'd seen the tiny stream of

bubbles rising at the same moment. He circled the leak with a white pencil and carried the tire into the garage.

The lady went to lean against her car. Danny followed her. A camper pulled into the self-serve island. "It's guys like these," Danny said to the lady. "They pull in and take 25 gallons a shot. With the holidays coming and everyone driving around, we'll never make it."

The lady looked at her nails.

Danny looked at the lady. He wanted to tell her about his dad. How he'd taken Danny and his mom out to dinner one night and just left them there. He didn't even pay the bill. Danny really didn't remember the incident. He was only three. But he imagined he could. Could picture the whole scene:

They were fighting. Here Danny was unclear, so he made up different arguments — his dad's late nights, his mom's shrill voice, Danny's bed-wetting. (That he wet the bed until he was 13 he never told anyone.) Anyway, they argued until his dad stood up and looked straight at Danny's mother, her make-up smearing around her face. He put on his jacket, and said, "Well ain't that the living end, Louanne."

Sometimes he remembered that his mother threw a glass after him. It hit his father's thick shoulder hard then bounced and shattered. His dad just grabbed his shoulder, didn't look back and kept walking. Other

---

times Danny remembered only that he wished she'd thrown that glass.

Today, when his father called, Danny thought about the glass. That he wished his mom had thrown it. And he wanted to ask this lady with her sunglasses and clean perfume, "Why do you figure he called now, twenty years later?" Somehow she looked as if she'd know.

The lady slid her smooth white hands into the pockets of her navy jacket. "So how much gas *do* you have left?" she asked.

"About four inches, 600 gallons, and with these trucks coming in I just know we're going to run out."

"Danny, this lady doesn't care about your problems." Mike was yelling from inside the garage. He couldn't have heard them, but Danny got the message and went out to help the guy in the camper.

Later that night as Danny sat in a House of Pancakes waiting for his father, he thought of the lady in the white Peugeot. He didn't know how to think of his father so he thought of the lady. Her smooth hands. He was drinking black coffee from an orange mug and rolling the corner of the paper place mat.

"He said he'd be here at eight," Danny said to the waitress, who'd come by for the third time to see if he was ready to order. "Let me just wait another 15 minutes. It's only twenty after."

"I just want to see how my kid is doing," Danny's father had said on the phone. "My pal." Said he was in town for a gig, had a few extra bucks that maybe Danny could use. Danny knew his father had sent money to his mother now and then, nothing regular. "And he wasn't worth going after," his mother always said. But this was the first time he'd called Danny directly. Danny thought about the money. Tried to guess how much.

Danny wasn't hungry, but he ordered a patty melt and fries because the waitress seemed to want him to.

"Still no sign of him?" she asked as she brought the order.

"No. That's my old man, though." He laughed, calibrating his voice to sound light. "He's in the music business. Unpredictable. Probably can't break out of his session. Sometimes they go all night."

"Yeah, that's when they drift in here. I know their likes." She winked. Danny bet she did.

The orange and turquoise decor of the Pancake House made the Christmas decorations, and all their forced cheer, seem out of place. The green wreaths, gold garlands, and fake tree with its red balls and winking lights felt insincere.

Danny paid the bill and drove his '72 Cougar back to the station. Mike would still be working and Danny didn't want to go home. As he idled at a red light, he

---

84

listened to the motor. The eight cylinders rose and fell, purring, low and constant. Predictable. He liked that.

When he drove into the station, he saw the sign: "NO MORE UNLEADED." Mike sat behind a window that was painted with holly leaves and a Season's Greetings.

"What are you doing here?" Mike asked when Danny entered in a gust of cold air. "I thought you were supposed to see your old man."

"Yeah, well it just didn't happen. I see we ran out. Can I help?"

"No gas, not much to do. But hang around. Be my guest." Mike was drinking a Pepsi and looking at a *Penthouse.*

It was cold outside and inside the glass-walled room. A dry cold typical of December in the Valley. Danny jammed red, chapped hands into his jacket and sat on the torn green vinyl couch across from Mike. Mike always sat at the desk. Danny smelled the stale cigarettes from the ash can at his elbow. Cigarettes, gas and grease, familiar smells. He always noticed them more in the cold.

"Whewee! Would you look at this honey." Mike whistled and flipped the magazine back so Danny could see "Valerie" on pink satin. His fingers left grease marks on the page.

"Nice," Danny said, hardly looking.

"What's wrong with you. You queer or something?"

"Nothing. I'm just sitting here. OK? Is there some law?"

"Hey, your old man. That's what it is. Forget your old man. What's he ever done for you?"

"Nothing. He's a piece of shit."

"That's right, a piece of shit. Now say it again: 'My old man is a piece of shit."

Danny smiled and repeated, "My old man is a piece of shit."

"Now together," said Mike, and they both sang "My old man is a piece of shit."

"Louder," yelled Mike.

"My old man is a piece of shit."

"That's right," Mike was screaming. And they chanted the chorus louder and louder until their laughter stopped them.

"And whenever you think of that loser, say that to yourself. Say that to him next time he calls say 'you're a piece of shit.'"

Christmas was two days away and even though the rain came hard, the streets and the gas station were jammed. Danny hustled from car to car. Vehicles filled with kids loose from school and packages, mounds of boxes, bags and bows. He was helping a woman in a brown Buick when he saw the white Peugeot. The lady